ANARCHISM

FOR BEGINNERS

ANARCHISM
FOR BEGINNERS®

BY **MARCOS MAYER**
ILLUSTRATIONS BY **SANYÚ**

FOR BEGINNERS®

an imprint of Steerforth Press
Hanover, New Hampshire

For Beginners LLC
62 East Starrs Plain Road
Danbury, CT 06810 USA
www.forbeginnersbooks.com

A For Beginners® Documentary Comic Book
Copyright © 2008

Cataloging-in-Publication information is available from the Library of Congress.

ISBN # 978-1-934389-32-4 Trade

Manufactured in the United States of America

For Beginners® and Beginners Documentary Comic Books® are published
by For Beginners LLC.

First Edition

10 9 8 7 6 5 4 3 2 1

Anarchism Revived

After the fall of the Berlin Wall in 1989, the rebellion against an unjust world found an opening within the anarchist tradition. The State was revealed as an enemy of liberty. And the libertarians were reborn. The anarchists left as their primary legacy an anti-authoritarian spirit that remained within the culture after the second World War and today has new formulations in theory and in practice.

There are many that think the anarchist movement belongs only to the 19th century, with some resonance in the 20th, but that history has passed it by both in doctrine and in political practice. Today however, it seems to be regaining its former strength, reorganizing, and emerging as a valid alternative for those who believe its history is not over yet.

1

The anarchists' fundamental belief is that the State or Government is the primordial tool of the oppression mankind has endured throughout history and the reason it is necessary to create ways of living in solidarity and freedom.

Little by little, the texts of Kropotkin, Proudhon, and Malatesta are regaining a relevancy that looked to be lost in the bottom of the barrel of time. And they're leading to new formulas with significance today.

Global versus universal

In activism against globalization (the Buy Local Movement for example), different anarchist organizations are playing a role in an effort to tip the scales, whether its preparing petitions against multinational companies or using the internet to transmit their message.

In reality, the economic side of globalization consists, basically, of getting work done in the cheapest place (usually Third World countries) and selling products where the concentration of wealth is highest. Anarchism has plenty to say about this.

Also, militant liberals apply themselves, dedicate themselves to smaller protests, and to no less affect, by supporting self-management in factories, for example, and promoting worker's unions.

Anarchism has been an active participant in squatter's movements and in the fight against the abuse of recreational drugs. In short, anarchism has been rediscovered to do battle against oppression on various fronts.

Sights set on power

PRISON CONTINUES, ON THOSE WHO ARE ENTRUSTED TO IT, A WORK BEGUN ELSEWHERE, WHICH THE WHOLE OF SOCIETY PURSUES ON EACH INDIVIDUAL THROUGH INNUMERABLE MECHANISMS OF DISCIPLINE.

MICHEL FOUCAULT

Although he never declared himself openly an anarchist, the French philosopher Michel Foucault contributed, in recent times, a different concept of power that seems to have taken hold in various rebellious groups that attacked different fronts at the same time.

For Foucault, power not only oppresses but produces a certain type of wisdom and control. This presence of power as something that goes farther than just repression made him think of the necessity of finding a way out of this net covering everything. He found it in the private sector; in some ways, the same way some anarchists set their ideas in their federations and communities.

NOAM CHOMSKY

WHAT IS IT THAT ATTRACTS YOU TO ANARCHISM?

IT INVOLVES A CHALLENGE TO THE MONSTROUS INSTITUTIONS OF COERCION AND CONTROL; THE STATE, THE PRIVATIZED TYRANNY THAT DOMINATES THE WORLD'S ECONOMY.

Foucault was not the only contemporary thinker to find inspiration in the anarchist position. Others include some who look to the libertarian texts for a starting point to reimagine our society completely. Such is the case for American Noam Chomsky, who has openly declared he is an anarchist.

Chomsky continues to be one of the intellectuals most critical of the politics of his own country, and has been steadfastly opposed to the United States' invasions of Afghanistan and Iraq.

Web of Webs

These intellectual contributions were made at the same time that a more spontaneous movement of different groups that attached themselves to anarchistic ideals because they no longer saw solutions in the political system and they were disenchanted with the world around them.

The discourse of anarchism has united various causes: that of environmentalism, feminism, the institutionalization of the mentally ill and the treatment of prisoners in jail. As if there were a new need to incorporate all the increasing complexities of society.

At a certain point, it appeared the thread of anarchism would be cut short. The anarchist movement, having risen from the fiery fight for social justice in the 19th century, was interrupted by the advent of Fascism, Nazism and the consolidation of Stalinism that surrounded World War II.

ADOLPH HITLER

JOSEPH STALIN

The secret of power is total domination of the government.

This concurrence of powers that reached into every aspect of life, not only obliterated millions of lives, but also a culture and an ideology. Anarchism, which up to that juncture had experienced notable growth, fell in the middle of the fight. It would be a half a century before it was revived and resumed its path.

Proudhon, the pioneer

The foundation of anarchism is a book titled *What is Property?*, published in 1841. In that work, the Frenchman Joseph Proudhon raises his opposition to any relationship based on economic benefits and postulates that the social contract upon which liberal ideology is based is a charade. The concern should be to preserve one's autonomy when confronted by social inequality and pressures of the State.

In these two famous phrases we find the summary and the seeds for the basis of anarchist actions. And its destiny. The search began with Proudhon, both to achieve the abolition of the State and to find new ways to ensure a just and free society.

Proudhon proposed the basis for what was called theoretical anarchism, in the context of the people's revolution that spread across all of Europe. With the ideas of the French Revolution of 1748 only half-fulfilled, people took to the streets, first in 1830 and again, more intensely, in 1848.

The general feeling was that equality continued to be just out of reach and that the system of political representation was another method of perpetuating injustice. In this climate of discontent, the works of Marx were born, on the one hand, and the works of anarchists on the other, and are the two forms that social protest would take through history.

Bankers without fortune

After the revolution of 1848, Proudhon continued to preach anarchism in several Parisian newspapers, where he launched his plan to set up a bank that would give laborers low interest loans and in this way generate and encourage industrial enterprises that did not depend on a boss.

Proudhon's purported mutualism was reflected in how the Bank of the People functioned. The scanty interest rates that were charged were enough to cover basic costs, but his example didn't catch on and spread.

Despite becoming a deputy of the people, Proudhon's opposition to the government of Louis Bonaparte led the authorities to throw him in prison for three years. There, he thought of a plan for government. By way of the people that visited him, he distributed it to various political parties and persons. But he was unable to break the indifference which the powers that be always held for anarchist projects.

In any case, Proudhon knew that his intentions were doomed to failure. His iron-willed opposition to political parties and the political system forced him to maintain independence, or be tied only to isolated projects such as the Bank of the People.

Proudhon took issue with the revolutionary strategies of 1848. But he always maintained his opposition to the State and any form of property, whether it was private or collective, just as the Communists suggested.

JOSEPH PROUDHON

Many have seen a utopian perspective of anarchism in the works of Proudhon. Like all pioneers, first he set goals then he tried to find ways to achieve them. In these first steps of anarchism, political action was barely a theme.

Unlike other anarchists, Proudhon believed that family and marriage should stay the same as they had been historically. He felt the same way about discipline.

All attacks on the family are a desecration to justice, treason against the people, and against freedom—an insult to the Revolution.

In light of this view, so different from the trajectory of anarchists who came after him, it is clear that Proudhon thought only in terms of political organization; to put it another way, he was convinced that society should run its course, without an external authority to interfere with the private sphere.

Criticisms by Marx

The arguments of Proudhon began to become popular with the working class. Marx - who met with him in Paris in 1844 — responded to his book, *The Philosophy of Misery*, with another whose title says it all, *The Misery of Philosophy*, where he launched furious attacks against anarchist tenets.

The principal criticism Marx had of Proudhon was his rejection of the idea of class struggle and his failure to identify the workers as the vanguard of the revolution still to come. For Marx, Proudhon used vague categories to interpret society and didn't recognize the true agents for change. This distinction would stand for decades.

Mikhail Bakunin, the road to revolution

The appearance on the scene of the Russian Mikhail Bakunin marked a new stage in the struggle between anarchists and marxists. He was born in the province of Tvar, in 1814, and his parents wanted him to follow a military career. Three years after he started his studies, he was already an officer.

THIS ISN'T FOR ME.

SO WHAT WILL YOU DO?

STUDY, TO THINK UP A DIFFERENT COUNTRY.

MIKHAIL BAKUNIN

While failing to adapt to the demands of barracks living, Bakunin quickly discovered other paths of study, specifically the study of philosophy, and especially that of Hegel, which is another source, along with liberalism of anarchist doctrine.

Little by little, his ideas converted him into a political agitator. He had to go into exile, but his struggle continued. In 1844, he undertook a trip to Germany, where he became intensely politically active. And even though he is absent from Russia, he is stripped of his aristocratic titles and condemned to life in Siberia.

Building on Proudhon, Bakunin added, both theoretical and doctrinal innovations, as well as revolutionary mystique and fervor. If the libertarian society was Proudhon's concept, for Bakunin it was a reality he urgently wanted to bring to fruition.

The State, the oppressor

Because of his sentence Bakunin chose France as his next destination. There he had meetings with Proudhon and Marx, from whom he distanced himself because of his ideas of a leading role for the proletariat, though they all agreed on the rejection of private property. For Bakunin, any form of the State would be an oppressor.

THE STATE IS THE AUTHORITY, THE FORCE, THE BRAZEN, AND THE INFATUATION WITH FORCE!!

These differences marked the entire relationship between anarchism and marxism. Lenin said that "anarchism is reactionary," while the libertarians believed you could not replace a dictatorship led by the bourgeoisie with one headed by the proletariat because power always corrupts.

To be against the State was, for Bakunin, to also be against war, which was always the consequence of the oppression of one class by another and the eventual exportation of that conflict over the borders.

THEY ARE GOING TO FIGHT FOR PEACE.

WHILE THERE IS GOVERNMENT, THERE WILL BE NO PEACE. THERE WILL BE TRUCES, SOME LONG, SOME SHORT. ARMISTICE FOLLOWED ALWAYS BY A STATE OF MILITANT BELLIGERENCE.

War meant, in addition, the moment when the State weighed most heavily on the people's lives, and for anarchists, it meant a way of defending the interests of the privileged using the people as cannon fodder. This political pacifism is another mark Bakunin left.

Voting still falls short

Bakunin also mistrusted the validity of representative democracy given the power differential between the classes. The vote, as it operates in a liberal society, is a way to validate the structures of power and continue to do everything as it is, without affecting the root of oppression.

This position marked a definitive difference between Socialists (who thought that the parliament was a political space to conquer) and anarchists. The difference also hides an attitude: for Socialists, any path to power is valid; for Bakunin, there should be complete consistency between ideas and practice.

Bakunin's revolutionary career participating in the organization of the militant anarchists, spans other European countries: Czechoslovakia, Prussia, Poland (where he was received as a hero). In Dresden, Germany he was taken prisoner and eventually deported to Russia.

I'M GUILTY OF FOLLOWING AN INFINITE HORIZON, WHOSE END NO ONE CAN PREDICT.

MIKHAIL BAKUNIN

Despite his almost constant exile, Bakunin's legacy is strongly linked to the situation in Russia. He began his revolutionary career denouncing what was happening in his country.

The revolution that came in from the cold

By asking for a confession from Bakunin, the czar commuted the sentence of the death penalty imposed by the German courts. These confessions, which were uncovered in 1912, included qualified denouncements by Bakunin himself, once he was out of Russia, as an unpardonable transgression for an anarchist.

In Siberia, he married Antonia Kwiatkowska, daughter of a businessman and twenty five years younger. Many biographers of Bakunin believed that Antonia was a bad influence and that she pulled him away from revolutionary life during his time still living in Russia.

Bakunin earned a living, first giving private tutoring, and later as a salesman. The relative freedom he enjoyed allowed him to resume, in parts, some of his revolutionary projects.

The very possibility of moving beyond the state's custody led him to plan his escape, which he did, by boat, first to Japan, then to California, ending up settling in London, where he starts to write his master work, *God and The State*.

The Conquest of Europe

Having been away from Europe for twelve years, Bakunin made up for lost time. First he engaged in Poland's struggle for independence from the Russian empire, but the expedition failed. Then he found a fertile place for his ideas: Italy.

The fraternity is clear in its platform: opposition to the state and religion. In 1867, the Congress for Peace and Freedom convenes, which includes, among others, the poet Victor Hugo. There, Bakunin met Garibaldi, while ideas he'd conceived increasingly gained favor with the youth.

He'll pass the ensuing years, between agitating and disseminating his ideas. But his health suffered while his pessimism grew due to the defeat of the Paris Commune and discussions with Marx. He left for Bologna to participate in the rebellion and, somehow, find a dignified end.

He traveled to Switzerland. His health deteriorated. He put on lots of weight and had trouble walking. Asthma makes life difficult for him, even when resting. His memory is no longer what it was. He studies philosophy and listens to Wagner, although he continues to admire Beethoven the most.

The end is near. Doctors diagnose him with a variety of diseases. He no longer can stand up and does not even have the strength to eat. Finally, he died on July 1, 1876, at three in the afternoon.

MIKHAIL BAKUNIN

The eternal solitude of death will not be the definitive end. On the contrary, after his death Bakunin's work begins spreading throughout the world and his ideas increasingly attract followers. He becomes the flagship anarchist thinker whose value is recognized even by an adversary as staunch as Marx.

Infinite Freedom

Following Marx, Hegel, and the teachings of their dialectical method of thesis, antithesis and synthesis, Bakunin believed the progress of man is achieved in stages.

History consists of the progressive negation of Man's animal nature.

Based on the method of Hegel's dialectic theory, which is also the starting point for Marx, Bakunin concluded that humanity will inevitably move towards a new form of society.

Another feature of Bakunin's thought is intense atheism, one of the marks he left on anarchism, which is fiercely antireligious and which influenced Dostoyevsky, who adopts his line of thought on God.

If God exists, Man Is a slave; Well now, the man Can And must Be free: Therefore, God does not exist.

The rejection of any form of religion, which Bakunin considered one of the faces of oppression, will win over vast constituencies, including Spanish & Italian campesinos, who have a long anticlerical tradition. In Buenos Aires, for example, the newspaper *El Burro* was launched in 1930—an illustrated newspaper devoted almost exclusively to mocking the Church.

But, without a doubt, one of the salient features of Bakunin's proposal was his idea of freedom, on behalf of which he justified anarchist's actions. It was never an individual's freedom, but always a freedom based on solidarity.

My freedom is a function of freedom for everyone. Oppression of some is the direct corollary to slavery for others. I am only free myself when I recognize another's humanity and freedom.

With this ideal, not always prominent among historians of anarchism, Bakunin's political belief, based on an ethic of solidarity, proposed a concept of freedom that overcomes all individualism: One is only free in a free society.

MIKHAIL BAKUNIN

The idea of collectivization as the means of production brought Bakunin close to communism's ideas. Hence, the difference must be clarified. It is not a question of imposing equality from above but it must be the decision of the entire society.

Here the door opens on the discussion. Should we wait until the citizens become aware on their own or must we address a political militancy? What are the means that will be debated and implemented within the history of anarchism? From violence to propaganda, from unions to elections.

Kropotkin—
The Libertarian Prince

Peter Kropotkin (1842-1921), like Bakunin, was born into Russian nobility, though he carried the title Prince. He also chose a military career, but his true passion was for geography and exploring. He went so far as to explore the fjords of Finland and Switzerland for the Russian Geographic Society.

PETER KROPOTKIN

Since his youth, Kropotkin carried a deep respect for science, and it helped shape the basis of his political views. He soon entered the political sphere and was immediately drawn to Marxism. At the First International, he arrived as a Marxist, but switched to anarchism and left ready to follow Bakunin's ideas.

Kropotkin took part in the first difficult discussions between socialists and anarchists, in which they appeared to share an enemy but not the same method against that enemy. It is no coincidence that a Russian like Kropotkin, as with Bakunin, would want to incorporate the peasants in the struggle.

PETER KROPOTKIN

For Marxists, the sections of the people that were not included in the working class became members of the so-called lumpen proletariat. That is to say that their destiny was to accept what the class that by nature opposed the regime - the proletariat — decides to be policy while at the forefront of the revolution.

Everyone's Needs

Kropotkin suffered the same persecution and imprisonment of his predecessors in anarchism and is regarded as one of the founders of anarcho-communism, with its proposals for communal societies and soup kitchens.

This is the fundamental difference between Kropotkin and the Marxists, for whom the social standing is defined by one's position in relation to production. Therefore, they proposed the slogan "to each according to his ability." For an anarchist, one could not distinguish what part of the social product belonged to everyone, therefore, the only just principal was simply to allocate each with whatever was needed.

Kropotkin joined the Russian Revolution of 1917, but soon his dissidence, or his non-conformity with Lenin and the Bolsheviks made him move away from the political scene to such an extent that his funeral in 1921 is considered the last public act of anarchism in the Soviet Union.

Kropotkin tried to maintain a critical distance from the Revolution, without overtly attacking it. He thought things should not go backwards, but rather the arrival of communism should be accelerated, that is to say, the dictatorship of the proletariat should be brought swiftly to an end.

Kropotkin's contribution to the theory of anarchism is his efforts to substantiate and solidify libertarian ideas, and to associate them with the latest discoveries of his time. Therefore, he defined anarchism scientifically as a universal concept and not just a societal reclamation.

For Kropotkin, anarchism is grounded in, accepted and discussed alongside the scientific concepts of the era. This quality also had its questionable aspects. Kropotkin supported the Allies in the First World War, which was widely criticized by Errico Malatesta.

PETER KROPOTKIN

Kropotkin's call for mutual aid lets him set forth anarchism as a moral doctrine, one that is radically anti-individualist. Which leads him to oppose the collectivism or communalism that Bakunin endorsed. In Spain there was heated discussion between the followers of both thinkers.

Finally, Kropotkin's project would be put into practice in Catalonia, until the end of the Spanish Civil War through a project of community life, with the slogan of "From each according to his ability, to each according to his need."

There have always been anarchists

Prior to the foundations of modern anarchism, there were other proposals and utopic societies that aimed to protect men from the oppression of the State. Among the very first, were the beliefs of the libertarians in Taoism and the separatists of the Stoics.

The Stoics, and their predecessors, the cynics, rejected the laws of man and proposed living in accordance with nature. Somehow, whether by conscious rebellion or by default and stubbornness, they never took part in public life and created communities of absolute egalitarianism, totally classless.

Attempts by communities to be independent of the State continue throughout the Middle Ages. Several religious sects are organized outside of the papal hierarchy and are subsequently persecuted as heretics. Among them, those of the Waldenses and Albigensians.

These sects often organized around a teacher and were more opposed to the hierarchy proposed by the Church than refuting any aspect of Christian dogma. They lived in communities or guilds and were self-governed.

Utopias and good intentions

With the advent of industrial society, there were a number of attempts to find solutions to the growing exploitation of man by other men. The utopic socialism of Fourier, the creator of small communities of self-management, was born.

For Fourier, an admirer of the Marquis de Sade, civilization is the result of repression that destroys the best of human beings. He argued that the *falansterios* should adapt and give in to passions rather than combat them. He also proposed abolishing monogamy.

For the Marxists, Engels disqualified Fourier's utopian socialism and the anarchists viewed the *falansterios* as a fantasy without handholds in reality and no chance of being implemented.

Anarchists, unlike the adherents of Marxism, recognize in both their pre-decessors and the utopian socialists, above all, the need to address education and their quest for the liberation of human beings to go beyond the purely economic realm.

William Godwin, a reverend without a church

Another predecessor, who held a lot of weight, especially for Proudhon, was the Englishman William Godwin, who in 1793 put forth his libertarian ideas in his book *Enquiry Concerning Political Justice.*

The State is looking for general well-being for all, but not through innovation, instead with a timid reverence for the decisions of our ancestors, as if it were natural to degenerate instead of evolve.

WILLIAM GODWIN

Godwin brought liberal positions to the extreme, revealing that anarchism proposes to bring about that which liberalism views as only theoretical, that is to say, freedom and equal rights. The obstacle to fulfilling this in practice is, precisely, the State.

Despite his religious activity, Godwin confronts the beliefs of the Church. He is obviously a man of contradictions; when the poet Shelley flees with his daughter, he prohibits them both from entry into his house.

MARRIAGE IS A LAW, AND ONE OF THE WORST LAWS. TO BE MARRIED IS TO BECOME SOMEONE'S PROPERTY, AND THEIR WORST PROPERTY.

A PRIEST SHOULD NOT BE SAYING THOSE THINGS!

WILLIAM GODWIN

Godwin's passion is reflected in these moments of opposition, but also in his contention that Reason is the highest value of humanity. Kropotkin said of him: "His conclusion was communism, but he did not have the courage to maintain his views."

Godwin's ideas are reflected in the intellectual and artistic, to the point that the English poets Southey, Coleridge, and Wordsworth decide to leave for America to build a society based upon Godwin's principles, a project that eventually failed.

This attention, however, did not help his thinking get taken as a starting point for the first anarchists. Bakunin did not know him, and his ideas were never taken up—perhaps because he himself did not seek a channel to implement them.

Clear differences

However, Godwin is the first to establish a clear distinction between the State and society, an idea that will be fundamental for Bakunin and for many of the paths that the anarchists will travel in their march.

THE SOCIETY WAS BORN FROM OUR SOCIETIES. THE STATE WAS BORN FROM OUR PERVERSIONS. THE SOCIETY IS GOOD; THE STATE, AT BEST, IS A NECESSARY EVIL.

WILLIAM GODWIN

Will the anarchists of the late Nineteenth Century join the list of Godwin and his predecessors, noted for ignoring any critique of political economy, proposing lucid formulations for social struggle, but not going beyond doctrine?

Max Stirner—
Or the Revolution for oneself

The German Max Stirner (1806-1856), whose real name was Johann Caspar Schmidt, is the creator of what is known as "individualist anarchism." He is the author of *The Ego and It's Own*.

THE STATE HAS A SINGLE GOAL: TO LIMIT, DOMINATE, AND OBJECTIFY THE INDIVIDUAL, SUBORDINATE ANYTHING IN GENERAL.

BUT TO LIVE IN SOCIETY, YOU MUST ACCEPT SOME RULES.

THE ONLY RULE IS MY OWN!

MAX STIRNER

Many anarchist historians reject his membership in the movement. However, Stirner—whom many accuse of being nihilistic, and whose influence was acknowledged by Nietzsche—had great influence on supporters of violent action.

For Stirner, it is a question of attacking everything that is opposed to the will of the individual, and the grandest obstacle that must be fought is the State. In it is subsumed all the shackles that impede the development of one's personality.

That position led him to reject any collective action and no longer recognize the proletariat as an agent of history, although he was a witness to its birth and its consolidation as a class. His greatest desire was to remain separate from any form of connection, whether social, economic, or political.

I and I alone

Stirner was not only consistent with this assertion of his message—the day of his marriage they had to go looking for him at a
house where he played cards - but he raised the idea of a society
in which the individual would be fulfilled as he chooses, without any
kind of bonds or obligations to others or with any kind of morals.

You could say that Stirner elevated narcissism to a philosophical
category. But even those who criticize him for this recognize that
he took the idea of freedom to its most extreme, even if it is the
absolute opposite of Bakunin. Which goes to show that anarchism
allows for internal discussion and that it shouldn't be treated as
a monolithic ideology.

ONLY IN THE MOMENT OF SELF AWARENESS AND NO LONGER SEARCHING WITHIN, AM I REALLY MY OWN PROPERTY AND ABLE TO ENJOY MYSELF.

IN FRONT OF THE MIRROR.

Time for action

Proudhon, Bakunin, and Kropotkin laid the foundations of anarchist ideology. Their opposition to the State, the Church and all forms of oppression, be it economic or social, soon echoed among workers and European peasants.

The work of propaganda was intense and fruitful; in a few years, there were multiple publications—many of them ephemeral and almost always persecuted by censorship—many meetings, and with them the followers of libertarian ideology. But that was only part of it. The concern of Bakunin was always that they not only maintain a state of mere protest.

The problem was to implement these ideas, seeing as how anarchism was opposed from the beginning to the idea of a traditional political party and participating in elections. Proudhon had himself planted this impossibility.

This refusal to join in politics as well as in the traditional Marxist idea of setting up a party of the proletariat not only produced great discussions within the hearts of anarchists but it was also opening the way to several alternatives, some greatly creative.

The union is strong

Between 1862 and 1864 there were meetings between followers of Proudhon and English union representatives who came up with the idea of the International Association of Workers.

But this attempt to coordinate the efforts of all revolutionary forces would end in a clash between anarchists and socialists that would be historic and would have tragic consequences, such as the killing of Kropotkin's followers by the Soviet regimes.

Bakunin believed that non-central countries—Spain and Italy—were the best places to spread anarchist ideas. For this reason, he sends an Italian to Barcelona who does not speak Spanish but is of a great expressiveness and holds to his convictions in any trial, Guiseppe Fanelli.

Fanelli showed great organizational capacity, to the point that in a few years, the Spanish anarchist movement not only became the largest in Europe but exported their ideas to the American continent.

Differences between Bakunin's anarchists and the Marxists deepens as the *International* develops, leading to the final break in 1872.

MARXIST:
Worker's Party.
Conquer the State.

ANARCHIST:
Small Communities.
Total Abolition of the
State and its power.

These discussions revealed not only two different strategies but also that the idea of anarchism over power was incompatible with socialism. For Bakunin, power always corrupts and every man, revolutionary or not, if he gets into the government, is a dictator in the making.

This is not a minor difference, and its implications go beyond politics and involve a different concept of man. Not coincidentally, for anarchism, the State not only exercises power but it oppresses. Man can only reach his full potential without the existence of authority.

This question is still pending after the failure of the Bolshevik system. Can one exercise oppression in the name of a revolutionary ideal? Can a new society be founded without any state apparatus?

The anarchists' inheritance

In the long history of libertarianism, a body of doctrines has been produced that stands as a legacy that grows in intensity each time it is revisited.

Proudhon: "Society must rest on contracts created freely between the interested parties. Freely!"

For Proudhon, it is not a single contract, as proposed by Rousseau, but the celebration of unlimited contracts, which meet the multiple needs of individuals.

The contract is not abstract but concrete. To put it another way, anarchists are opposed to the fiction of a "free society" and they want to arm society from the bottom up. To replace the other great fiction, the State, anarchists propose federations.

"Unlimited contracts to be held at all levels—individual, professional, regional, national and even international-that for the act of being treated freely guarantees the freedom of individuals."

The federalist formula, as demonstrated by the experience of the Commune in France, only works when it is universal. This complicates its difficulties. Tolstoy, Bakunin, and Proudhon himself, had already comprehended this.

Federalism, however, appears as the only way to guarantee both justice and liberty, concepts that at least during the existence of the Soviet Union appeared to be contradictory.

While federalism was a system of multiple and permanent contracts, it did not clearly define the issue of social organization.

How to live in Society

Max Stirner, preoccupied by the idea of a society that exists outside of us (that is to say something that we can not change) and that oppresses individual motivation, generated the idea of partnership.

As Stirner did not consider the absolute freedom of man possible, he saw in this form of organization a safeguarding of our identity, which Stirner himself gave the name "the association of the selfish."

For Proudhon, discarding the rule of the State raised the question of the flow of goods. To confront this, he proposed two things: to replace money for credits based on work and to establish labor cooperatives.

This is called mutualism, which dissolves the hierarchies in connection with work and with money. His idea is preserved in the current cooperatives and mutual aid societies.

The Banquet of Life

Finally, Bakunin marked a change from Stirner and Proudhon, according to whom man could not survive without property. He proposed its abolition, because it was born of injustice and helps perpetuate it.

FIESTA SEGÚN RENOIR.

The social problem is, for Bakunin, a matter of poor distribution of wealth, and communism would bring all the solutions. In turn, work will become something agreeable as men would not be oppressed nor dependant on the salary.

These solutions reveal some basic ideas that distinguish anarchism from other revolutionary movements. Essentially, the concept of power as utterly negative in all its forms.

POWER MONSTER EATING SMALLER POWER MONSTER.

Power is fed by power and cannot do anything except perpetuate itself.

This leads Bakunin, for example, to reverse the Marxist idea that division into classes is what breeds the State, and seeing this as the culprit of all social inequality. What we have to do is to break the vicious cycle of oppression of the majority by the minority.

Neither God nor Love

Power not only corrupts those who exercise it, but also those who suffer under it. The choice is clear: to be slaves or rebels, but while there are those enslaved, one must be at their side.

It is clear who is responsible for this despotism: authority, property, and religion.

The matter of religion marks another great anarchist contribution.

To think of God as the sustenance and producer of power is something different from thinking of the opiate of the people, as Marx said.

To attack God is to attempt to liberate oneself from ultimate Love, as Bakunin proposed — it is to aspire to an absolute freedom that recognizes that there is no other authority besides man's.

Leo Tolstoy, above all, Peace

At the same time that debate was raging, anarchism began to expand its perspective. In Russia, along with Kropotkin, Leo Tolstoy proposed his version of nonviolent resistance to the State and oppression.

"If one one hundredth of the energy spent by the revolutionaries had been spent searching within their own spiritual selves, they would have dissolved this evil against which they have fought so hard and still they fight, in vain."

LEO TOLSTOY

For the author of *War & Peace*, the change begins within yourself, and oppression is a question that must be resolved, first and foremost within your own conscience. It is a moral choice that isn't explained in terms of politics nor by radical activists.

You could say that Tolstoy followed a line of thought that had more to do with what was seen as sentiment in anarchism—he adhered to statements regarding community that dated back to the very first Christians—more than supporting the continuation of the ideas of Bakunin or Proudhon.

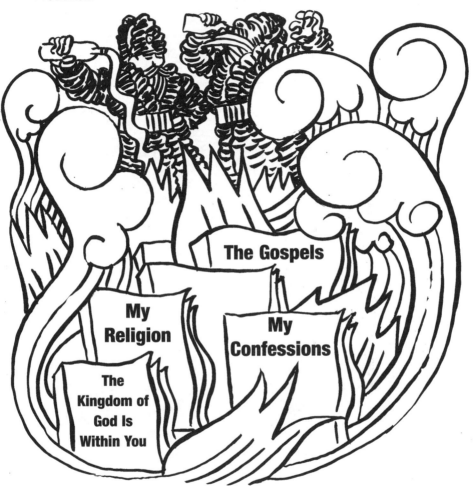

This Russian author, born into aristocracy, suffered a crisis of conscience that almost led him to suicide. The crisis came when he compared his economic situation, well-off and rich, to that of the rest of his town, where most lived in miserable poverty. Thus he rediscovered primitive Christianity and writes several books to that effect, many of which were censored.

Tolstoy renounced his home and his wealth when he was eighty-two years old.

He made himself peasant clothes, and even made his own footwear. He fell ill on a train and finally died on an iron platform, in the train station manager's office.

While some orthodox anarchists dismiss Tolstoy as not really part of the movement, he did make a contribution. More than anything through his decision to self-sacrifice, to live by his principles, and suffer the same scarcities as his neighbors. Although his contribution to history cannot be reduced simply to this, his was anarchism put into practice rather than just theorizing.

War, but above all else, Peace

For Tolstoy, the existence of the State was incompatible with the practice of Christian doctrine. The political hierarchy trampled the equality that Jesus preached. This brought about a form of anarchism that some called the Christian anarchists.

ONE MUST REJECT ANY FORM OF THE STATE, WHETHER IT'S ABSOLUTE MONARCHY, THE CONVENTION, THE CONSULATE, THE FIRST OR THE SECOND EMPIRE, CONSTITUTIONAL MONARCHY, THE COMMUNES OR REPUBLIC.

LEO TOLSTOY

By affirming his position this way, he was trying to leave any obstinate persistent clutching to "unintelligible dogmas, moreover, useless ones," and recuperate the teachings of Christ, whose essence is Love, an altruistic love, forsaking all ego and lasting even after death.

This opposition without exception against all forms of power led Tolstoy to condemn property and wealth, despite his birth and social standing, coming from one of the most elite families in Russia and at the time of his conversion he was one of the most famous writers of his country.

But, in principle, his teachings were not directed at the oppressed—who knew the situation full well—rather aimed at softening the hearts of the powerful, who had "the lives of the rest of us in their hands."

To confront these ills, Tolstoy proposed passive resistance and conscientious objection. In this respect, many see in him the predecessor to Gandhi's actions in the process of gaining freedom for India from the English crown.

MAHATMA GANDHI

Never act against love.
Do not resist evil with acts of violence.

There was contact between the two men. In 1910, Tolstoy wrote to Gandhi, telling him that his militant pacifist fight "is the most important activity being carried out on the earth today."

The impossible Peace

But this was not the path that anarchism would follow for its expansion. For one thing, there was enormous agitation work that reflected itself in the almost permanent presence in newspapers and publications that defended the libertarian ideas.

In general, these publications, which didn't correspond to any particular group, were scanty in duration and often victims of censorship. But their persistence in journalism demonstrated the value that anarchists placed in debate and the distribution of information.

Tolstoy's idea, and that of many other anarchists, was for the creation of a new distinctive society. Anarchism would convert itself, little by little, into the ethics of human relationships, based on solidarity and on the rejection of society's laws or impositions.

This was an attitude already present in Proudhon's initial intentions and his Bank of the People. Even in the context of oppression, the idea was to generate new ways of living together, far from all selfishness. An anarchist doesn't divide his public life from his private conduct.

Anarchists, about things

But there were many who were not willing to wait for the moment of final freedom, and so they undertook direct action to shake up the conscience of the people. If the enemy is power, we must go against it.

Opposition to the idea of progressive convincing opened the doors to what was called direct action, the use of violence, completing isolated acts, destined to wound those in power and generate pre-revolutionary conditions. There's something in the air this time, that will give legs to these notions.

Errico Malatesta:
from Italy comes unity

Italy would be the first place where the anarchist's political fight would turn out to be the most intense. There, Errico Malatesta (1858-1932) proposed the necessity for political organization and founded, in 1899, the International Party of Socialist Anarchism.

With its strong militancy, anarchism entered into its expansion stage, as we've already seen in Spain, but now also crossing over to the American continents. In one of his habitual exiles, Malatesta traveled to Argentina, where he collaborated in the founding of what would turn out to be the most important libertarian movement in South America.

While a student of medicine, Malatesta first aligned himself with the socialists of the First International where he met Bakunin and adhered to his principles of anarchism. He was the principle instigator of direct action.

In this way, Malatesta set in motion a series of strategies to disperse the libertarian politics, among them expropriation of lands from the richest sectors. This made certain popular bandits and bad guys very sympathetic to anarchism.

The triumph of Will

Malatesta did not believe, as Kropotkin did, that the advent of anarchism was the result of scientific research and reasoning, rather he contended that in order for it to materialize it requires a will and permanent militancy.

Actions like permanent militancy tried to break free from the schema of the political parties and follow more closely the motto of the First International: "The emancipation of the workers will come from the work of the workers themselves." The gamble is on the spontaneous reaction of the oppressed to the State.

In accordance with these ideas, Malatesta took part in numerous popular insurgencies, in Spain and in Belgium. In this way he was putting into practice the idea of internationalism in the anarchists' cause.

ERRICO MALATESTA

The strategy for these protests was to construct – with the protest itself as the vehicle – alternatives for emerging out from under the oppression and to establish ties that would bring together the anarchist society. There isn't a single moment in the revolution that changed everything overnight.

Salaries, never again

Malatesta was also the driving force behind so-called "communist anarchism," pushing for the construction of a society without classes and some sort of synthesis with Marxism, though skipping over the stage of the dictatorship of the proletariat.

A NEW MORAL CONSCIENCE WILL BE FORMED, WHEREIN A SALARY WILL BE REPUGNANT TO MEN, THE WAY SLAVERY AND THE INQUISITION ARE REPUGNANT TO MEN NOW.

ERRICO MALATESTA

The solution the Italian saw was through the idea of federations, loosely and freely grouped that would respect the tendencies of the populace and get together to solve specific problems. Malatesta feared the exercising of power and wanted a complete change in the human condition.

With this policy, Italian anarchism was converted into a fearsome force for Fascist Italy. Mussolini sent Malatesta to prison, but the respect he felt for him prevented him from executing Malatesta.

It's not a coincidence, this respect and at the same time aversion. The Fascists knew that Malatesta was a powerful enemy, but also that he was highly esteemed by the people. To execute him would have launched a series of protests that they sought to avoid.

Malatesta died in prison, after passing through several exiles in France and in England, where he continued his tireless preaching in favor of the fight for freedom. He was always faithful to his idea that a new society would not simply come along on its own.

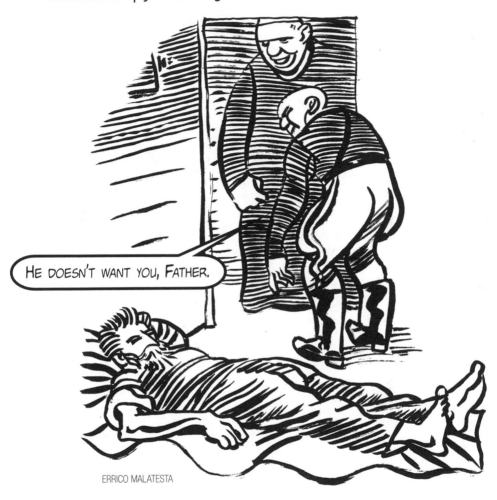

ERRICO MALATESTA

Errico Malatesta was a man of action, thus leaving only a few scattered writings. In one of them he speaks of love in free society, saying, "We'll eliminate the exploitation of man by other men, fight the brute pretension of a man who believes he owns a woman, we'll fight religious and social prejudices, assuring for every man, woman and child their well-being and their freedom, and then the only evils left will be the evils of love."

Anarchism in Spain

The second country leading the advance of anarchism at the end of the Nineteenth Century and the early decades of the Twentieth Century was Spain, where the peasants and workers strongly adhered to the libertarian ideals.

It was also in Spain that the anarchist movement endured for the longest time, from the beginning of the movement in 1868 to the end of the Spanish Civil War, in 1939, when they were persecuted by the Falangists.

This persistence may have its origins in a resistance to civil power and a raging anticlerical sentiment in the Spanish population, which had already suffered centuries of exploitation by landowners who found a powerful ally in the Church.

This perspective has led many scholars to see links between anarchism and the Millennium movement of the late Nineteenth Century, which proposed a return to primitive Christianity. Anyway, while there is a convergence of some ideas, the Millenium movement only made it as far as declaring itself, while the Spanish anarchist movement sought ways to put their ideas into practice.

Priests and Soldiers

Following tradition, the first Spanish anarchist movements took place in the rural areas of Andalucia, a region that mixed revolutionary impulses with militant ideals.

But this unity was quickly broken and anti-clerical sentiment overcame the respect for Christian doctrines. Atheism would become a core value for Spanish libertarians, in this way continuing some of the liberal traditions.

To combat this movement the Andalusian Civil Guards fabricated the existence of an anarchist group called Mano Negra, whose alleged aim it was to kill the rich and powerful in the region. But in reality, it was just an excuse to crush the emerging revolutionary groups.

As often happens, those in power create confusion between crime and politics. In this case, the Spanish authorities were not too original. But it was in Spain that the relationship between rural bandits and anarchists showed itself most intensely.

It was also in Spain where an undercurrent is consolidated and given a name, anarcho-syndicalism, which in some ways recuperated an angle that the anarchists had lost sight of. They had not given much attention to the question of unions.

(FOR AN 8 HOUR WORKDAY — BETTER SALARIES!)

Thus, anarchism returned to the route of collectives and unions, after an era of propaganda that was criticized by its own libertarian militants as being too violent. Nonetheless, violence and militancy would be present in all the workers struggles throughout the early Twentieth Century.

The Spain of a fight and an idea

In 1906, a congress convened in Amsterdam where, after long discussions, the anarchists are accepted into associations. Malatesta ends up adhering to this new form of struggle.

The Spanish anarcho-syndicalism expanded in leaps and bounds. The National Confederation of Labor – CNT– united one million members at the beginning of the Spanish Civil War.

As a result of their struggles, the Spanish anarchists were brutally repressed. Rebellions that occur in Catalonia in 1909 are attacked by colonial troops brought from Morocco. Francisco Ferrer y Guardia, educator and activist, was arrested and executed in retaliation.

FRANCISCO FERRER

Repression did not prevent the growing membership of workers to anarcho-syndicalism, but rather the relentless fight created the foundation of the conflict that erupted in the Civil War, where anarchism occupied the first front against Franco.

Diego Abad de Santillan:
the search for common sense

The Spaniard Diego Abad de Santillan learned the principles of anarchism in a place that had become common for militant liberals: jail.

To avoid military service, Santillan traveled to Argentina, where the anarchist movement was very strong. From there he traveled to Germany, and returned only after meeting several other revolutionaries.

DIEGO ABAD DE SANTILLÁN

Upon his return, Santillan helped form the FORA (Federación Obrera Regional Argentina), one of the strongest anarchist groups on the continent and protagonist of thirty years of revolutionary struggle.

The FORA published one of the most enduring newspapers of the anarchist movement, *The Protest*. Santillan brought to the movement a legitimate concern over creating syndicates, trying not to fall into the trap of mere vindictive fighting.

First in line

Santillan finished defining something that was only hinted at in Bakunin's political strategy; defining the role of minorities in the various struggles undertaken by workers in the first decades of the the Twentieth Century to gain better working conditions.

THOSE MOST ENLIGHTENED MILITANTS MUST BE THE FIRST TO LEAD OTHERS BY EXAMPLE IN THE STRUGGLE.

DIEGO ABAD DE SANTILLÁN

Unlike Kropotkin, Santillan was convinced that civilians, their countrymen, are not by nature anarchists and militants, and so the anarchists themselves had to lead by example to convince them of their ideals. The militant anarchist is converted, as happened in the Spanish Civil War, into a hero and a martyr for his cause.

It became evident then that the anarchist ethic is not just theoretical, as we saw in Tolstoy, for example, but that the principle of solidarity was arrived at through fighting. With these principles in hand, Santillan returned to Spain in 1931.

In effect, exile gave him time to reflect on the need to adjust to new times. The spontaneous revolutionary era was over, those in power had signaled that anarchism was an enemy to be handled carefully. You can be optimistic but some hazards should not be left to chance.

Santillan takes a position as Minister of Economy with the Generalitat. At that time, collectivized industry was at its peak, but we'll get to that a little later.

DIEGO ABAD DE SANTILLÁN

WE CANNOT CONTINUE WITH THE OLD WAYS OF THE ECONOMY. WE MUST UNDERSTAND THE COMPLEXITIES OF THE NEW ECONOMICS AND ADOPT THE METHODS OF THE ENEMY.

These words not only show the drama of the situation but also the perception that victory was possible. The fact that anarchism was suppressed from the left and the right (as happened in the Soviet Union) is an indication that this wasn't a movement linked to just one circumstance but rather was destined to endure.

In 1937, Santillan had a decisive meeting, intervening to promote the surrender of anarchist forces in the Spanish Civil War. Later, back in Buenos Aires, he would regret this decision.

WE SHOULD HAVE FOLLOWED THROUGH TO THE END. THE BIGGEST CAUSE OF THE FAILURE OF THE REVOLUTION WAS THE POOR QUALITY OF LEADERSHIP, AND I INCLUDE MYSELF IN THAT.

DIEGO ABAD DE SANTILLÁN

Maybe, as Bakunin said so many times, the militant anarchist, with his demands on the self for purity, and his faith in humanity, has committed errors for which he will pay dearly. The methodological discussions that we've seen show that the doctrine is not to be valued just for itself, and perhaps anarchism had not found the best way to spread. But some ways were worse than others.

Men carrying bombs

At the end of the Nineteenth Century and at the beginning of the Twentieth Century, along with the rise in organized groups, came isolated groups promoting another kind of action; bombing. In this anarchist era, the movement became synonymous with terrorism, and its presence caused fear in the halls of power.

Although other organized anarchists refused to condemn these attacks, Malatesta's position was that any action should be framed in a political strategy. The general feeling though was that these were impulsive individuals, whose only ambition was to destroy symbols of power.

The ideologue and initiator of this trend was the Russian, Sergey Nechayev, who after meeting Bakunin, met with a group of youths in St. Petersburg to further conspiracies. This was easy to do in the political and social climate of his country, wavering in uncertainty and the loss of old values.

SERGIO NIETCHAIEV   MIKHAIL BAKUNIN

The proposal was linked with the state of uncertainty for the Russian intelligentsia that didn't establish clear boundaries between a political strategy and a nihilistic view of the world, whose sole objective was destruction.

Revolutionary Catechism

Nechayev wrote "Catechism of A Revolutionist," which some say was approved by Bakunin himself (something that the majority denies) and that was sent to his disciples as a guide for action. It detailed a range of actions aimed at achieving the revolutionary goal.

1. Defame powerful people, by any means, even lies.

2. Commit all necessary assassinations.

3. Make a common cause with bandits who are outside the law.

4. Rob and steal to get the necessary means.

The Catechism, whose very name revealed confusion between religious duty and political militancy, launched a series of sects in Russia that were devoted to constant attacks. This example would shortly be followed and expanded upon beyond Russia's borders.

Nechayev himself implemented this catechism, these orders. He killed a friend he suspected was an informer. Then he fled to Switzerland, but was extradited back to Russia. He died in 1872, after ten years in prison in St. Petersburg.

Few cases in history show what Nechayev did, both a theory and a model for systematic terrorism. Maybe therein lies the explanation for the fascination his contemporaries held for him, even among those who didn't adhere to anarchist ideas.

Dostoyevsky was inspired by Nechayev and his companions to write one of his best known novels, *The Demons* (which tells the story of a group of violent anarchists). Their fight goes down in history with the name nietchvaiévina.

THIS QUALITY OF LOOKING AT THE TRUTH IS PARTICULAR TO THE NEW GENERATION OF RUSSIANS. THE ESSENCE OF THE RUSSIAN REVOLUTIONARY IS THE NEGATION OF HONOR.

FYDOR DOSTOYEVSKY

Dostoyevsky's protagonist, Stavroguin, reflects the anxiety of the Russian intelligentsia, between a decomposing State, the injustices of the secular czarism, and the revolutionaries' promises. The same context that surrounded Nechayev.

On the brink of explosion

Persuaded that propaganda and the dissemination of ideas is not enough to impose the anarchist ideal, the Swiss Jura federation meeting at the Anarchist Congress of Saint-Imier in 1877, decided to endorse violent methods. This decision set off a terrible paranoia among European authorities.

The attacks happened. In Germany, a tinsmith and a doctor attack the emperor, a worker tries to kill the Spanish king, an Italian cook made an attempt on the life of the monarch. Isolated anarchist groups were called out as responsible for the attacks.

None of these men belonged purely to anarchism, nor were the attacks linked to any particular strategy. But the threat launched by the Anarchist Congress of Saint-Imier appeared as the major explanation for the bombs and assassinations.

Anarchism gained fame by these acts, but police vigilance was stepped up and the laws were more repressive. Nietzsche celebrated the forthcoming arrival of the nihilist era, when nothing would be sacred, nor would anyone obey any symbol of power or of wisdom.

The Violence and The Glory

The nihilist climate of the time meant that more attacks were received with satisfaction than with disapproval. Writers celebrated the actions of these groups. The French poet Laurent Tailhade wrote a fiery defense of one of the attacks, based on aesthetic reasons.

Who cares about the victim if the gesture is beautiful!

It was to be expected that Tailhade's writing was received as scandalous. But he did not retract his statement, even in the face of charges brought against him for "inciting murder." When the Czar visited Paris, the poet continued his defiance and so spent a year in jail.

Ironically, Tailhade was gravely wounded in one of these attacks; he lost an eye. And he wasn't the only one fascinated with violence, the novelist Jean Richepin joined in the celebrations.

"The poetry of these adventurers, these brave sons of the rebellion, for whom Society was almost a bad wetnurse, and who bite the flesh to calm their hunger..."

As the confessed heir to Baudelaire, Richepin was one of the innovators of popular French dramas, and a maestro venerated by Georges Brassens. As exemplified by Brassens putting his poetry to music, through which you can see a forgotten antecedent to a way of looking at the world that will only reemerge in the 1960s.

Dynamite and Guillotine

In this context, it's not surprising that the line between anarchism and crime began to blur. The story of Frenchman Ravachol is an example of this confusion somewhere between pathetic and comical.

Ravachol desecrated a tomb in search of jewels and murdered a devotee who had retired to the hermitage, suspecting that a fortune was hidden there. Trapped by the police, he began yelling, "I'll exterminate all the police to serve humanity." He managed to escape prison within the year before being jailed again.

Ravachol dedicated his time as a fugitive to planting bombs in the doorways of judges who participated in lawsuits against anarchists, and committed several other crimes as well. To escape again and again, he left notes declaring his suicide.

Ravachol is arrested by the police in a café where the owner recognized him. Avengers came and destroyed the bar, smashing everything.

The capture of Ravachol was the result of his ardor for anarchy. After being moved between several prisons, he was sentenced in front of a crowd of more than five hundred people who came to applaud. Because he posed a menace to judges, he was sentenced to death. His only response to the sentence, "Long live anarchy!"

It was his destiny to become a popular hero. Not only did many anarchist newspapers come to his defense, but anonymous singers composed songs to honor him that circulated among the people, transmitted by word of mouth.

But not everyone who was an anarchist shared in the fun. Sebastian Faure, one of the principal leaders, made public his concern over the consequences of the attack for his group. However, he did take Ravachol's orphaned child into his care.

Ravachol was sentenced to death by guillotine. After this, writers of his time considered him a hero who was sacrificed in the name of the good of humanity. Collections were gathered for the families of his accomplices.

His execution was carried out despite rumors of plans to free his accomplices and murder the executioner instead. The guillotine interrupted his last words, "long live the rev—" but his example left a mark.

Common ground: Death

The wave of attacks did not end. The mother of the Italian anarchist who killed the French president Sadi Carnot, received a photo of Ravachol with the caption, "He's in good company." In 1893, Auguste Vaillant threw a home-made, nail-laced bomb into the French Chamber of Deputies. It failed to go off and he was trapped inside.

Parisian nuns leave their offerings at Vaillant's tomb.

Vaillant also left his testimony for posterity. "Gentlemen," he said to the judges, "you will sentence me in a few minutes, but when I receive your verdict, I will at least have the satisfaction of having wounded society. I threw the bomb against those who are primarily responsible for society's suffering."

It was not long at all before the counterattack. The day after Vaillant's bombing, the first anti-anarchist law was passed. The French government persecuted the anarchist newspapers for inciting crime. The socialists opposed this new law and pointed to corruption in power as the reason for the growth in the anarchists' movement.

Jean Jaurés, the principal socialist deputy did not miss the opportunity to attack the libertarian militancy: "The day that the same boat takes away the anarchist assassin and the political mercenary, takes them to the fiery land of exiles, they will stand in front of each other like two complementary aspects of the same social order."

Another consequence of the harsh repressive laws was that, since then, anarchists were treated like common prisoners and locked in the same prisons with thieves and criminals of all stripes.

Anyway, although the authorities' idea was to confuse the two, in anarchism there is a special sympathy towards criminals. Bakunin himself said, "the criminal is the sole and genuine revolutionary, a revolutionary without fancy phrases, he is tireless and indomitable, a popular and social revolutionary, apolitical and independent of any State."

WILLIAM MCKINLEY

But laws could not stop the wave of attacks. Between 1893 and 1910 the following were all assassinated; Empress Elizabeth of Austria, the president of the Spanish Council Canovas del Castillo, King Umberto of Italy, and William McKinley, the president of the United States.

But police took advantage of this crime wave. A bomb planted in a procession in Barcelona was attributed to an anarchist group. Later it was revealed that it was an officer who placed it there to provide another excuse for repression. Malatesta argued that the time had not come yet for the People to take violent action.

Other paths

In fact, the terrorist nihilistic slant had isolated anarchism and we find this explored in the writings of Stirner, who saw crime as a form of expressing subjectivity.

THE POWER OF THE STATE IS MANIFESTED IN THE FORM OF COMPULSION; IT USES FORCE TO WHICH THE INDIVIDUAL HAS NO RIGHT TO APPEAL. IN THE HANDS OF THE STATE, FORCE IS CALLED "RIGHT"; IN THE HANDS OF THE INDIVIDUAL, IT'S CALLED CRIME. ONLY THROUGH CRIME CAN AN INDIVIDUAL DESTROY THE POWER OF THE STATE.

STIRNER

Although it's an ironic result, the logic of attacking was defensive. It worked to preserve the individual in the face of the State, affirming, through violence, that the two could not coexist.

There are other alternatives for those looking for a free society, which would only be possible through collective action. One of the more concerned with overcoming the necessity of terrorism was the Frenchman, Fernand Pelloutier (1867-1901).

As an alternative proposal, Pelloutier campaigned in favor of the general strike as a strategy. He imagined a country ground to a halt by its workers would soon see the fall of those in power.

Work to know

Parallel to propagandizing the idea of a general strike, Pelloutier worked as a secretary for the Labor Exchange, an institution that was designed to protect and secure employment for the unemployed. But it took it's role much further.

Ultimately the Labor Exchange was the place where workers could learn about what Pelloutier called, "The science of their misery," that is to say, the study of different forms of exploitation.

The Labor Exchange is the "university of the Worker" where we teach each other and learn to improve ourselves.

FERNANDO PELLOUTIER

The main beneficiaries of the Labor Exchange were the sons of workers, who sought to convey their pride in manual labor. Socialist Georges Sorel knew better than anyone how to define the spirit of this innovative project.

To secure freedom in the future, we have to make the youth love their work. We must make them responsible, artists and scholars of everything that has to do with production.

GEORGES SOREL

Another project of Pelloutier's that did not happen was the creation of a Museum of Labor, through which he would show all the stages of the production process and the value of work.

The biggest concern was that the workers not believe in the necessity of the capitalists, that they classify them as parasites who made the State their host.

Pelloutier's own magazine, *Workers of the World,* was part of his goal to reveal the situation of workers in his country and the world. He was an encyclopedic type of anarchist who believed that the course of change began at the bottom.

Bulletin Board Rebels

One question that anarchists always asked was why, if power by definition is against the people, do the people continue to believe in those in power? Why do they obey? And one of the answers they found was in the educational system.

KROPOTKIN, MY FRIEND, WHAT DO YOU THINK OF EDUCATION?

IT IS ONE OF THE WAYS OF PERPETUATING OPPRESSION!

PETER KROPOTKIN

This conviction led to the need for educational experimentation. The pioneer in this was Frenchman Paul Robin, who founded the Prévost Orphanage in Cempuis, where he taught the trades and provided an anarchist education.

At the same time, Tolstoy inaugurated his Yasnaia Poliana School, where peasants were educated on their land, and through which he conveyed his libertarian ideas.

But the educational project where the anarchists had the most success was in Spain, under the hands of Francisco Ferrer y Guardia, who was the creator of the Model School, which had branches throughout Spain, Europe, and the United States.

Education for everyone

Ferrer (1859-1909) was a self-taught man whose curriculum reflected the education given at the time in Spain. And since that was dominated by the clergy; social discrimination, violence and religious prejudices abounded.

Faced with this educational policy, Ferrer armed a federation of free schools, which focused on broad, non-specialized education, without exams, and of course, absolutely secular.

The rejection of religious education cost Ferrer his life. In 1909, there was in Barcelona what is now known as the Tragic Week, a brutal crackdown on a protest questioning the obligation to participate in a raid on Morocco. Ferrer was identified as one of the instigators.

Despite international protests against what was clearly a fraudulent process riddled with irregularities, Ferrer was executed three months after the trial.

Ferrer's contributions would be seen in several pedagogical practices through the next century, such as trying to create a climate of freedom in the classroom, without authoritarianism, and helping students find their true path.

Among those who still follow this perspective, we can mention Paulo Freire, founder of the famous and questionable Summerhill School in England, and of the movement that objected to school, which in the 1960s and 1970s proposed not to send children to school at all.

STOP SERVING GODS AND EXPLOITERS. LET US LEARN TO LOVE ONE ANOTHER.

F. FERRER Y GUARDIA

Southern Latitude

New ideas came with the wave of emigration from Europe in the late Nineteenth Century, mostly workers from Italy and Spain arriving on the shores of Argentina.

The Argentinian oligarchy's initial enthusiasm for immigration was quickly replaced by rejection and fear. The journalist Enrique Rodriguez Larreta describes anarchism as "a hellish cult, which does not distinguish between homelands, nor institutions, nor individuals, because it is all confused under the same curse."

Their fear was somewhat justified. Anarchism grew strong quickly, pushed along by the momentum of Malatesta living in exile in Buenos Aires. And in 1896, the Great Railway Strike broke loose.

The strike ended in a ferocious takedown, which caused seven deaths and left more than thirty wounded. But it marked the starting point of anarchist participation in trade unions in Argentina that would extend through the 1930s.

Presidential tolls

The direct action brand of anarchism was also present in Buenos Aires. It is suspected that there were militant libertarians in the 1873 attack on Sarmiento. Even president Julio A. Roca would become a target in 1886.

PRESIDENTE J.A. ROCA

Another president, Manual Quintana would suffer an attack, this time by a revolver in the hands of the Catalonian typographer Salvador Planas y Virella in 1905. The assassination attempt unleashed a wave of persecution against local anarchists.

Those attacks had the logic of assassination so dear to Stirner's followers. But the act carried out by Simon Radowitzky on November 14, 1909 against the chief of police Ramon Falcon had other motivations.

Radowitzky was sentenced to life in prison in the Ushuaia jail, until he was pardoned by President Hipolito Irigoyen in 1930. The current police school is called Ramon L. Falcon.

The sequence of attacks and repression continued, though there were two moments of greatest tension. The first was the Tragic Week of 1919. A massive and spontaneous movement of workers occupied the city demanding improvements, after a strike in the workshops of Vasena.

The Patriotic League, a vigilante group composed of young people from the high society participated in the brutal repression. The magnitude of the protest, which surprised even the militant anarchists themselves, revealed the state of social tension.

The Patagonia tragedy

Two years later, a scenario unfolded in the province of Santa Cruz, in an episode that would go down in history as "The Patagonia Rebellion." It all started with a worker's claim filed in the zone and signed by Lieutenant Colonel Varela.

LT. COLONEL VARELA

Instructions for kits, ration of candles, salary of 100 pesos

But the British ranchers did not meet any of these requirements, which provoked the rebellion of the workers and the return of Varela, though this time in another spirit and with different orders.

Varelo unleashed a ferocious repression that culminated in the shooting of one thousand five hundred workers, some without trial, and with the blessing of Irigoyen and the British consulate.

Despite the protests that followed in Buenos Aires, nothing was investigated about what occurred in Patagonia, and Varela won the complete backing of the radical government for all his actions.

The German Avenger

On January 25, 1923 Kurt Wilckens was 37 years old. Aware of the events in Patagonia, and as a correspondent for two anarchist newspapers in Germany, he decided to take justice into his own hands. That day, he threw a bomb at Varela as he left his home.

Wilckens was caught at the scene of the attack and told the police, "It was I alone, the only author, I made the bomb by myself, without any help." With his legs broken, there was no trouble arresting him and taking him to jail.

A wave of vengeance swept back in. While he was in his convalescent bed, a man from the Patriotic League, Ernesto Perez Millan, entered his cell, dressed as an onguard officer.

In a moment in Argentine history in which justice was most absent, the memory of those anarchist avengers worked as a signal that things could be otherwise. That is ultimately one of the great libertarian lessons: History is never finished being written.

VARELA

NIÑA ANÓNIMA

KURT WILCKENS

Part of this history remained hidden until the investigative zeal of intellectuals like David Viñas and Osvaldo Bayer uncovered the forgotten. And the names of the fighters today regain their previous status.

Anarchism on behalf of women

Anarchism's peak intensity coincided with the struggle for women's suffrage. As the issue of voting was never relevant in libertarian doctrine, the subject of Women's Rights was never central until the emergence of Emma Goldman (1869 - 1940).

Goldman was one of the first in favor of birth control, which was illegal at the time. A Russian immigrant, she arrived in the United States after escaping from an anti-semitic pogrom, and very soon discovered the dark underbelly of "the land of opportunity."

Employed as a seamstress, she quickly realized the rigors of industrial work. But what really inspired her to turn to anarchism was the 1886 Haymarket protest, in Chicago. A bomb exploded during a demonstration and police arrested eleven anarchists.

Four of them were hanged, one committed suicide, and the rest remained in prison. Her outrage prompted the young Goldman first to join the unions' struggles and later to help publicize libertarian ideas.

OUR WOMBS WERE NOT BORN TO BE SLAVES EITHER.

EMMA GOLDMAN

BEFORE BEING ACCUSED OF A CRIME, YOU SHOULD KNOW YOU ARE HERE FIRST FOR BEING ANARCHISTS.

The Weaker Sex in Action

In her militancy, Goldman followed several paths. First she bet on violence. Her target was one of the repressors at the Homestead factory in Pennsylvania. Still famous today for her powerful public speaking and writing, at times, she even worked as a prostitute to get money for protests.

WE'RE LEAVING WOMEN OUT OF OUR FIGHT.

EMMA GOLDMAN

After failing in the armed attack, actually carried out by her boyfriend, Goldman actively participated in the campaign against the newly instated draft for World War I, which got her thrown in jail and subsequently deported in 1919. Her first destination was Russia, where the Bolshevik revolution had just broken out.

At first she was enthusiastic about what she saw, but Goldman became increasingly wary of the Soviet regime, until she rejected it completely. She wrote two books about her experience: *My Disillusionment in Russia* and *Living My Life.*

"Never before in history has the State been so strong, so reactionary and even counterrevolutionary, in short, the antithesis of the revolution."

EMMA GOLDMAN

Next she lived in exile in London, but her message there was met with indifference. In 1936, she moved to Spain to join forces with the anarchists there who were fighting against Franco's regime.

Despite often being isolated, in jail or in exile, Goldman dedicated her life to the women's cause, convinced that a real revolution should abolish inequality between the sexes. She declared what would be known as Women's Rights in society.

The right to have a personality. The right to refuse to have children if you don't want them. The right to refuse to be a servant to God, the State, your husband, or your family. Freedom from fear of public condemnation.

Today, the figure of Emma Goldman is seen as a landmark in the feminist movement, because she was able to raise women's place in society so far ahead of her time.

Sacco & Vanzetti–Solidarity

In the same fight against conscription that cost Goldman a life in exile, were two Italian workers – Nicola Sacco and Bartolomeo Vanzetti, who had also come to the United States in search of a new life and freedom.

Sacco and Vanzetti's expectations, along with those of their sixty colleagues, were not met, and so they returned to the United States. But some of that group believed in the need to keep attacking those responsible for the continued oppression of workers.

Soon, they placed a bomb at a prosecutor's office, causing an explosion of major proportions on Wall Street, September 16, 1920. The work of intelligence officers indicated that police should be monitoring Sacco and Vanzetti, among others.

A second occurrence led to the chief of police in Massachusetts immediately pointing to the anarchist cell as being responsible for the murder and robbery of the payclerks at a factory in South Braintree. Sacco and Vanzetti were arrested and accused of the crime.

An unjust judge

The judge assigned the case was prejudiced by the climate of paranoia that was at large in the United States since the libertarian attacks and the worsening social tensions.

JUDGE WEBSTER THAYER

Although the alibis provided by both men were valid, a series of maneuvers converted the trial into another form of retaliation for social protest. An inability to prove that the bullets were from Vanzetti's weapon, eyewitnesses that faltered in their testimony and other witnesses who were disqualified for speaking only Italian or poor English, all made up chapters in the highly publicized trial.

Finally, a death sentence was handed down. Vanzetti made an incendiary statement in response to the judge's ruling, one that he continued to issue from jail in letters sent to his family and friends and for which he is famously remembered.

> SOON BROTHERS WILL NOT FIGHT THEIR BROTHERS. THE CHILDREN WILL NO LONGER BE DEPRIVED OF THE SUN OR AWAY FROM THE GREEN OF THE FIELDS IN THE COUNTRY. THE DAY IS NOT FAR OFF WHEN THERE SHALL BE BREAD FOR EVERY MOUTH, A ROOF OVER EVERY HEAD, AND HAPPINESS IN EVERY HEART.

There was a six year battle to save Sacco and Vanzetti from the death penalty, at that time the electric chair. A man apprehended for other crimes said he knew who was really responsible for the deaths of the pay clerks. His testimony was never taken into consideration.

The triumph and the agony

At midnight on August 22, 1927, Nicola Sacco and Bartolomeo Vanzetti entered the execution room of the State of Massachusetts. They were placed in the electric chair while they waited in vain for the governor's pardon.

In 1971, the governor of Massachusetts apologized for the trial of Sacco and Vanzetti, and acknowledged that it was a ploy to bring down the workers' protests. The tragedy of the two Italian workers remains in history as a demonstration of how power will stop at nothing when it feels threatened.

Also in 1971, the film *Sacco and Vanzetti* premiered, starring Gian Maria Volonté, which snatched this terrible moment from history and was very successful on the big screen.

"The Ballad of Sacco and Vanzetti," performed by Joan Baez, one of the icons of protest music in the United States and part of the first Woodstock celebration, also enjoyed great success. Soon it became an anthem against injustice.

JOAN BAEZ

HERE IS FOR YOU, NICOLA AND BART
REST FOR EVER HERE IN OUR HEARTS
THE LAST AND LONELY MOMENT IS YOURS
THIS AGONY IS YOUR TRIUMPH.

The world would not stand by, impassive to this farce with tragic consequences. In just under a century of existence, anarchism had united mul-
titudes of workers, from all over the earth, from France to Spain to Russia, from the United States and South America. And from all these
places, protests were heard.

The episode galvanized international solidarity and showed that not
everyone was compliant in the apparent absence of social justice since
the First World War. It generated a peaceful, almost festive atmosphere
so that some even called it the "Belle Époque."

Land and liberty

Anarchy had the opportunity to put its ideas into practice in Spain, during its Civil War between 1936 and 1939. That era went down in history as the Libertarian collectives. It all started when workers with their own militia managed to defeat the fascist forces.

The victory allowed the farmers and workers to keep their land and factories when the fascists retreated. There the idea of collectivization was born, with decisions made in the popular assemblies convened by the powerful CNT (National Confederation of Labor), anarchists with a membership of a million and a half strong.

These assemblies were a new way of organizing society and work. At the same time, farmers and peasants abandoned old ideas about law and property.

Those who did not have anything to give to the collectives were admitted regardless, with the same rights and obligations as others. The intention was that there would be no hierarchy among members stemming from their previous histories.

Be your own Boss

They formed work groups, with a minimum of five men, and all were required to perform some task. The constitution of the groups was decided on by the members themselves.

Each group elected a delegate that participated in the assemblies, which in turn had administrative commissions and management committees. The delegates were responsible for obtaining materials, the exchange with other zones or areas, and public works, such as building schools.

A traditional enemy of Spanish anarchists became unthinkably useful. The ample, ventilated spaces of churches served as storage facilities. There, all the products from the countryside and industry were stored.

The commune members received a salary, following Kropotkin's principles, to each according to his need. Some collectives established a family wage, and in others, the wage was not paid in cash but in goods. And in others, one could take, unrestricted, what one needed, from food to cigarettes.

The freedom of others

The working age was expected to be from fourteen to sixty, guaranteeing the feeding and care of the others. There were some complaints from women who received a lesser salary than men, especially in the country.

The integration of collectives, unlike what happened in Russia, was not mandatory. The only requirement for each individual was that one could not possess more land than what one could work and one could not employ anyone outside the family. It was a way to maintain the anarchist principle that there is only freedom where all are free.

The functioning collectives and their expansion across Spain put into question the old idea that men always aspire to more than they have.

The collectives did not produce what is known as capital accumulation. They consumed what was necessary and, if there was surplus, it was sent to other places that did not have those goods. There were also workers moving from region to region where help was needed.

Along with the collectives there was a modernization of farming methods and experimental farms were established. This generated an increase in production by almost fivefold during that time period.

The literacy campaign was just as intense. Education followed the principles of anarchist Francisco Ferrer. Also, libraries, cinemas, and community centers were built.

Take this!

The collectives were destroyed when Franco triumphed, and its main leaders were prosecuted and imprisoned. Thus ended one of the most interesting experiments in popular organization, though there would be a resurgence of sorts later, in the hippie communes.

With the end of the Spanish Civil War, anarchism began to fade from the political landscape, all but extinct except for a few samples of its tradition and pride.

Beyond some anarchist newspapers that continued to publish and some anarchist figures sprinkled around the world, there was one final "swan song," associated with freedom.

In 1944, the contingent that liberated Paris was integrated with Spanish anarchist soldiers, active combatants in the National Front led by Charles de Gaulle. Riding in on a tank—The Guadalajara—they were the first to enter the French capital, as told in Ernest Hemingway's account.

But it is true that, beginning in 1930, anarchism started to lose standing throughout the world. Perhaps the main reason was the place it occupied then against the State. The State not only ruled over life in countries with fascists and regimes, but even the so-called Welfare State quickly showed its limits and contradictions. Even its most ardent supporters, like German philosopher Jurgen Habermas, noted this.

FOR EXAMPLE, THE STATE HELPS A TROUBLED FAMILY, BY GIVING THEM A PSYCHOLOGIST, ISN'T IT VIOLATING THEIR FREEDOM?

JÜRGEN HABERMAS

The difficulties of societies organized around a state power provoke the anarchist spirit and so it continues in other areas, especially in the cultural realm, where the aim is to escape from any guardianship.

Artists without a System

Beyond the obvious sympathies some artists share with anarchism — you can add to Tolstoy, the cases of Oscar Wilde, Aldous Huxley, and the Argentine Alberto Ghiraldo — there is something that transcends mere affiliation with an idea or a party.

Picasso's response can be understood as a rejection of any art agenda. And he made this statement in an era when artistic manifestos were typical and mainstream.

Since 1920, on the one hand, Futurism, led by Italian Filippo Marinetti, and on the other, Surrealism, whose leading figure was Frenchman André Bretón, shocked audiences with their new proposals.

These vanguards — with their praise of individualism on one side and technology on the other — ended up associated with political powers. Futurism, with its passion for war, holds fast to Italian fascism, while the main components of Surrealism ended up integrated into the Communist party.

Philosophy in the Cabaret

Along with these movements, there emerged a group who denied any method and who's very name reveals the refusal to be trapped in any social convention: Dada.

These meaningless words were spoken in an arena that sought to destroy all significance of language. As if they had taken Bakunin's formula to the realm of art: "All construction is first a deconstruction."

The Dadaists were searching, through their nonsense, for the haphazard appearance of a new reality, different from the tragedy in which they lived.

"From within a detested society, and ruptured open from it, Dada appears as the only society in which life is possible."

It is no coincidence that one of the major Dadaists, Hugo Ball, was the German translator for Bakunin's works. The anarchist spirit, who's complete rebellion led to its disappearance, survives in this form at the forefront of new movements.

In another situation

The cunning of certain ideas is that they've pretended to disappear and then, when it's least expected, they reappear. Just as anarchism was continued by Dada, Dadaism was part of a secret plot.

The Situationist movement, led by Guy Debord in Paris in the 1950s, took Dada's nonsensicalness to the extreme. A black projection screen with absurd dialogue on it was his signature piece.

His next act was to attack Charlie Chaplin when he visited Paris to promote his film, *City Lights*. Considered by many as the greatest promoter of sentimentalism, the Situationists made it clear where he was not wanted.

Underappreciated and viewed with contempt as eccentrics in the beginning, the Situationists did eventually gain followers. Guy Debord theorized about the entertainment culture, where everything is pre-ordained and where freedom is only found outside of film.

The Show must NOT go on!

The Situationists left their role as provocateurs so they could disseminate information on their ideas for a post-war society. For them, "politics is a kiosk at the fair; culture, a roving corpse; the economy, a trick."

I TAKE MY DESIRES FOR REALITY BECAUSE I BELIEVE IN THE REALITY OF MY DESIRES.

With admission at the university level, the Situationists were one of the principal originators of the revolt of May 1968 in France. The students joined in with the proposals of this anti-capitalist movement that looked to abolish work.

The deeds of that May brought into practice the Situationist ideas of creating new situations, outside of the logic of entertainment-based society, where everything is created to venerate power.

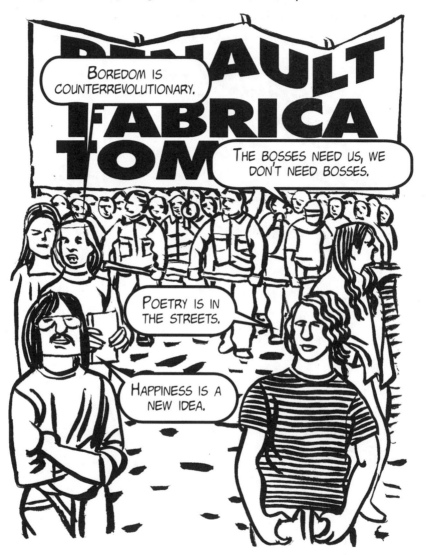

One of the main legacies from May 1968 is the multitude of slogans that continue to pop up to surprise us, even today, many of which are rooted in anarchist ideals: "Neither God, Nor Love." "Destruction is the joy of creating." "Freedom for others adds to my own freedom."

Demand the Impossible

The spontaneity of the movement in May 1968 took the government by surprise, and their retaliation was therefore especially strong in the streets of Paris, taking over factories and universities where there was any sign of uprising.

The movement continued in other parts of the world, in the United States as opposition to the war in Vietnam, and in Latin America for democratic governors.

While the events of May 1968 seem to have left no obvious political consequences (the Right continued in power), the new ideas that arose from there were marked with the same two problems: how to address power and freedom.

For Foucault, power relations in communism in the Soviet Union and in China were the same as any in Western society, in all their references to the family, to work, to sexuality and education.

For the other figure in what is called post-structuralism, Gilles Deleuze, freedom is limited by societal demands that we have a certain identity determining the course of our lives.

NEITHER METHOD, NOR RULES, NOR RECIPES, ONLY A LONG PREPARATION. INSTEAD OF RESOLVING, ONE SHOULD RECOGNIZE AND JUDGE, PULL AND FIND, STEAL.

GILLES DELEUZE

Ultimately, it's a question of finding a road to freedom that never ends, and that dissolves permanently into other identities, never to be what is expected of us.

Revolution and safety pins

This is the secret spin-off of anarchism, it shows itself next in the least expected place; the rock scene of the mid 1970s.

SEX PISTOLS, SINGER JOHNNY ROTTEN

The punk rock that emerged in England as a reaction to the languishing rock scene, took many forms of expression, anarchy among them.

Rock, which had started as a rebel movement, had settled increasingly into the business side of things, and many in the scene said nothing of what was happening with youth.

Punk came to talk about reality, as Pete Townsend said, the leader of one of rock's historic groups, The Who, "When you listen to the Sex Pistols and their songs, what will surprise you right away is that this is what's really happening."

God sink The Queen

The Punk movement was diverse in its attitudes (there were many discussions because some groups wore swastikas). And their fans did not have hopes of changing the world.

Their movement was about rejecting what was proposed, without suggesting alternatives. The world seemed a dark and complex place, though that didn't mean they didn't have serious problems with authority and the establishment.

The release of the album, *God Save the Queen* by the *Sex Pistols*, with a portrait of Queen Elizabeth II with her mouth crossed with a pin and a hook, and a punk version of the British anthem, led to new fans, rejections of, and a renewed look at, the world of hierarchies.

The Sex Pistols succeeded in delivering a clear message, thanks in part to the producer Malcolm McLaren, who continued with the Situationist message. He said, "To create, you first need to destroy. Destruction for creating is much more honest. The punks are bad, but they're not asking for an apology."

The reappearance of anarchist attitudes in our culture and thinking should not be considered a defeat but rather a symptom of when a system triumphs it only provokes discomfort. It's a malaise and unhappiness that is not resigned to silence.

RELIGION

EDUCATION

UNEMPLOYMENT

WAR

LACK OF OPPORTUNITIES

Current forms of anarchism, aware of this discontent, have recovered the joy and spirit of the struggle. They have also found ways to unite their beliefs with other groups of social protest.

A planet in danger

The environment is one of those fields, long a territory of the con-scientious. The American anarchist Murray Bookchin has managed to give a new twist to the problem of the planet's devastation.

SOCIETY IS AN ECOSYSTEM, IT CAN BE LIKE A POND, GUIDED BY THREE PRINCIPLES, UNITY IN DIVERSITY, SPONTANEITY AND COMPLEMENTARY, NAMELY, THE LACK OF HIERARCHIES.

MURRAY BOOKCHIN

In Bookchin's view, we establish hierarchies in the world of nature, (for example, "the king of the jungle") as a projection of how our own society functions.

Also, man's action runs parallel between society and nature. Society grows more bureaucratic and farther from nature, while nature grows less organic through mans' systematic destruction of it.

Bookchin's remedy to this situation is anarchy, which is not just synonymous with chaos, but an iron will not to compromise on principles that are so simple, and should be natural to us: cooperation, diversity, freedom away from the authoritarian scheme.

The world in our own hands

A new contribution, like Bookchin's, coincides with the need for anarchist groups today to unite with other just struggles for a better world.

Index

MARCOS MAYER is a journalist, professor and writer. He is the author of, among others, *Remendios del Paraíso*, (which won the Antorcha Prize), *The Essential Writings of Che Guevara, Ahora el Humor* (interviews with Argentinian comedians), and a critical text analyzing Ernesto Sabato's novel, *Sobre Heroes Y Tumbas*. He has written for a variety of print publications, and edited several anthologies. He teaches journalism at the Centro Universitario Devoto, a Buenos Aires prison where he runs a newspaper with the prisoners.

SANYÚ is the pseudonym of Hector Alberto Sanguiliano, an illustrator and cartoonist who has been published in the principal newspapers of Argentina since 1974. He has adapted literature to illustrated works, taught courses, been a judge of illustrations and comics, and organized two gallery shows of Argentinian comics and the history of comics. He is the author of *100 Years of Comics in the World*.

THE FOR BEGINNERS® SERIES

AFRICAN HISTORY FOR BEGINNERS:	ISBN 978-1-934389-18-8
ANARCHISM FOR BEGINNERS:	ISBN 978-1-934389-32-4
ARABS & ISRAEL FOR BEGINNERS:	ISBN 978-1-934389-16-4
ASTRONOMY FOR BEGINNERS:	ISBN 978-1-934389-25-6
BARACK OBAMA FOR BEGINNERS, AN ESSENTIAL GUIDE:	ISBN 978-1-934389-38-6
BLACK HISTORY FOR BEGINNERS:	ISBN 978-1-934389-19-5
THE BLACK HOLOCAUST FOR BEGINNERS:	ISBN 978-1-934389-03-4
BLACK WOMEN FOR BEGINNERS:	ISBN 978-1-934389-20-1
CHOMSKY FOR BEGINNERS:	ISBN 978-1-934389-17-1
DADA & SURREALISM FOR BEGINNERS:	ISBN 978-1-934389-00-3
DECONSTRUCTION FOR BEGINNERS:	ISBN 978-1-934389-26-3
DEMOCRACY FOR BEGINNERS:	ISBN 978-1-934389-36-2
DERRIDA FOR BEGINNERS:	ISBN 978-1-934389-11-9
EASTERN PHILOSOPHY FOR BEGINNERS:	ISBN 978-1-934389-07-2
EXISTENTIALISM FOR BEGINNERS:	ISBN 978-1-934389-21-8
FOUCAULT FOR BEGINNERS:	ISBN 978-1-934389-12-6
GLOBAL WARMING FOR BEGINNERS:	ISBN 978-1-934389-27-0
HEIDEGGER FOR BEGINNERS:	ISBN 978-1-934389-13-3
ISLAM FOR BEGINNERS:	ISBN 978-1-934389-01-0
KIERKEGAARD FOR BEGINNERS:	ISBN 978-1-934389-14-0
LINGUISTICS FOR BEGINNERS:	ISBN 978-1-934389-28-7
MALCOLM X FOR BEGINNERS:	ISBN 978-1-934389-04-1
NIETZSCHE FOR BEGINNERS:	ISBN 978-1-934389-05-8
THE OLYMPICS FOR BEGINNERS:	ISBN 978-1-934389-33-1
PHILOSOPHY FOR BEGINNERS:	ISBN 978-1-934389-02-7
PLATO FOR BEGINNERS:	ISBN 978-1-934389-08-9
POSTMODERNISM FOR BEGINNERS:	ISBN 978-1-934389-09-6
SARTRE FOR BEGINNERS:	ISBN 978-1-934389-15-7
SHAKESPEARE FOR BEGINNERS:	ISBN 978-1-934389-29-4
STRUCTURALISM & POSTRUCTURALISM FOR BEGINNERS:	ISBN 978-1-934389-10-2
ZEN FOR BEGINNERS:	ISBN 978-1-934389-06-5

www.forbeginnersbooks.com